"There are very few business manuals I've ever come across that can help you in
our business life and raise a smile a   te
ull Rodgers - she brings life and grea   a
erious subject. If you don't already l   ur
hristmas or birthday wish list!"
hn Highfield, Magazines Editor, She

GW00371280

My Grandmother always used to sa   as
wasn't that common. Well Kate's b   es
easy for everyone to get better at what they do and have more fun at the same
me. A joy to read or to dip into."
ndy Veares, Area Director, HSBS Bank Plc

wish I'd had this book when I was doing my MBA. It would have made the whole
xperience a lot more enjoyable."
acey Gillott, Chief Executive Officer, Lincoln Pelican Trust

This is a book I'd give as a present to a business colleague. There is humility in the
riting, which I found appealing...The cheerful, positive, intelligence of the author
omes through on every page."
he Self Publishing Magazine

Kate's approach is unique, refreshing and enjoyable – simple, clear messages
ommunicated in a way that holds the reader spellbound."
nda Hardie, Executive Director and Depute Chief Executive Finance and IT
esources. South Lanarkshire Council

Punchy and powerful, this book fires home the message that having fun, being
appy and loving your work isn't the icing on the cake, it is the cake."
hilip Howells, Project Manager, Lloyds TSB Plc

This book is great. I have experienced Kate speaking at a couple of events and this
ook supports everything she says. The book is brief but everything within these
ages is key to the way that we work today. Bring humour into the workplace -
es absolutely! I would strongly recommend this book to everyone who wants to
ake their work life more interesting and fun!"
ill Bolton, Managing Director, GEB Solutions

find this book, in a word; GREAT...I dip in and out of it on a very regular basis. I
ork in the stress fuelled world of real estate - much of the time it is all rush, rush,
nd more rush. Pearl of Bizdom reminds me to take a minute, slow down and gain
ome perspective. I highly recommend it."

ue McArthur, RE/MAX Real Estate, Canada

Kate's words PEARLS OF BIZDOM are really quite light, but like the real thing, a
evelation shining bright. Funnily enough it is a SERIOUS business tool, Buy it and
elieve it because you're no fool."
ensions Officer, Warwick County Council

About the author

Kate Hull Rodgers is managing director of HumourUs Limited, Europe's foremost experts on Humour in the Workplace. Over the past 15 years her advice has been sought by businesses, governments and health organizations in 29 countries on 5 continents.

Kate has devised a series of speeches and training programs specifically for British business on the strategic use of humour. The demand has been overwhelming. Presented in an "enter-training" way, her seminars make even the stiffest upper lips quiver.

Her background combines expertise as an award winning comedienne and playwright with experience in the mental health system. **Cracked Up**, her testimonial play, told her story of being hospitalized for a year. During her treatment she underwent intensive therapy, received a cocktail of drugs and was placed in full body restraints – chained to the bed.

Much of the healing humour and motivational work she has developed draws from the lessons learned during her recovery.

HumourUs' clients include numerous blue chip and multi national companies, as well as many public sector organizations. Kate's work is the subject of ITV's documentary *Laughter is the Best Medicine*.

Originally from Canada, Kate now lives in England with her actor husband, Bill Rodgers, and their two sons, Harvey and Dominic.

Pearls of Bizdom is Kate's first book. Visit her at www.humourus.co.uk

Pearls

of

Bizdom

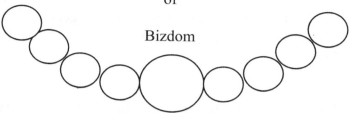

Kate Hull Rodgers

HUMOURUS LTD
United Kingdom . Canada

Pearls of Bizdom

By

Kate Hull Rodgers

ISBN 978-0-9557481-0-3
HumourUs Ltd
Peek-A-Boo cottage
3 Church Lane
Blyton
Lincolnshire
DN21 3JZ
ENGLAND

Printed and bound by Biddles Ltd. King's Lynn. Norfolk

www.humourus.co.uk

Dedication

To Bill, my partner in life, business and laughter.
To Harvey, the answer to all my hopes and prayers.
To Dominic, my miracle baby.

Thank you

To Pamela Anthony for editing this book. Thank
you for making my voice clearer and our friendship
even dearer.

Foreword

Read this book carefully, and heed my Health Warning. It could change the way you do business.

Kate Hull Rodgers is a remarkable woman. And she approaches management matters from a completely different point of view than most of her peers. She also practices what she preaches, and that was why we met.

As an unsuspecting editor of a regional newspaper I hadn't realized that my attendance at a worthy dinner had been clocked and she had talked the organizers into letting her sit next to me.

It therefore seemed perfectly natural that at our first meeting our conversation turned to newspapers in general and business columns in particular. I fell for the bait and she slowly reeled me in.

Thus started a long association which had Kate writing a regular column in the quirky, but pithy and often disarming style that became her hallmark.

Kate's comments on commercial and business life are based on good sense and good judgment. When the columns first appeared in the paper I had letters from business readers asking who on earth was this woman who dared to tell them how they might improve their business performance? And with humour? Had I gone mad?

Slowly the letters began to change. The very people who had been critical were being converted as they realized that Kate's columns actually made good sense. And people could have a bit of fun on the way.

Where do her ideas come from? My guess is that they come from a nimble mind which has absorbed, filtered and interpreted her wide experience of life with all its trials and tribulations. Kate's triumph in the business world is no overnight success. It is honed from years of experience, experimentation and knowledge. Her mind is like a sponge which soaks up information then wrings it out in a very special way. Kate's way.

Alan Powell, Editor of Sheffield Newspapers Ltd.

Introduction

"Have you got a book, Kate?"

If I had a penny for every time I have been asked this, I would indeed be a rich woman. My answer has been: Yes, I've got a book, I just haven't written it yet.

Why not? After 20 years of teaching workshops and seminars, I have enough material to fill a small library. So, why no book?

My plethora of excuses begins with lack of discipline, closely followed by fear of putting my thoughts in print.

You see, I'm a speaker, a performer. My words live on the wind; it's very scary to have them permanently placed in ink. Much of my work is testimonial; I learn something everyday, so how could I possibly etch my thoughts in stone?

But now, it is the eve of my 45th birthday; a time of reflection. In my life, I have created many things, in many genres - plays, speeches, businesses, babies, homes, training courses. It is now time to create a legacy that is more than just memories and ephemeral moments. I am finally ready to write the book.

Fortunately I do not have to start from scratch. You see, three years ago, in a 'Must get writing if I am ever to write a book' frame of mind, I began to look around for opportunities to write.

I began with what I was reading at the time: the Sheffield Telegraph Business Section. Would I, could I, dare I contribute to this respected voice of my local business community? I would, I could and

I dared. I was given the opportunity to write a monthly column. I called it First Friday.

What a revelation! Writing was a joy! I had something to say and people were keen to read it!

After two years of writing First Friday, my husband Bill turned the question; "Have you got a book, Kate?" into a statement. "Kate, you've got a book."

"Have I?"

Yes, I have.

Pearls of Bizdom is a collection of my First Friday columns; reworked and re-edited. They document how the trials and tribulations of every day life can teach us lessons for success. These lessons are universal, and show how easy it is to go from 'grit to great'.

Enjoy!

April, 2006

Contents

Kate Hull Rodgers

Kate Hull Rodgers

PEARL OF BIZDOM
1

PEOPLE WHO HAVE FUN
GET MORE DONE

It is hard to believe I make a very good living encouraging enjoyment in employment. It is harder to believe we have allowed our workplaces to become places where my services are in demand.

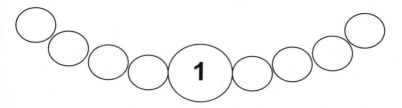

Why Humour, How Humour

At HumourUs our slogan is "Learn the Worth of Mirth and Laugh all the Way to the Bank." Short, sweet and to the point. But still many prospective clients ask; "What is Humour in the Workplace?" and "How will we benefit?"

These questions don't surprise me. When the Institute of Management in the USA surveyed managers in 24 countries to determine workplace priorities, results revealed that British management placed 'fun at work' lower than any other country. British businesses often have a target driven, "get your head down and get on with it" workplace ethos. No surprise then that stress is now the number one reason for absenteeism. ILL, I think, is an acronym for I Lack Laughter.

Humour in the Workplace is a strategic approach to increase efficiency by increasing employee enjoyment. The aim is to have fun and to make work more like play.

The benefits include measurable improvements in communication, teamwork, morale, stress levels, and staff retention. Training budgets are positively affected as research shows that happy people learn more quickly and profoundly. The links between employee well being and a healthy bottom line are increasingly recognized in the modern workplace.

Each person in an organization has a unique "sense of humour". The challenge is to find a strategy that includes different kinds of fun which appeal to the diverse tastes of a workforce. Recognizing that our sense of humour can be developed is important. Our humour response is a learned behaviour. It is affected by our gender, age, religion, culture and upbringing. The goal of Humour in the Workplace is to find a workplace ethos that encourages all the individual senses of humour to create an organizational vision of allowable fun. Not just allowable, but encouraged.

This fun may manifest in many simple ways – participating in charity functions, celebrating birthdays, socializing, exchanging humourous communications, having a lottery syndicate, serving healthy snacks, flexible working hours, dressing down, caption competitions, sporting events, DVD lunch hours, in house jokes, motivational training…

Too often these initiatives are thought of as extra curricular. Humour works best when it is woven into the fibre of how we work. The aim is for fun to become a benchmark of a business's success. This can be aided by some strategic input, which is when I get brought in.

As a humour specialist, I teach the benefits of increasing humour and then design a humour program tailored to each workplace. These are unique 12 step programs, so unique they only have 10 steps.

Embracing the organic fun that is already

happening will account for at least 2 steps. I then develop another 10 steps to create a strategy to learn new humour skills. This helps to train the different individual senses of humour to respond positively to the same stimuli. Shared humour leads to an organizational ability to collectively accentuate the positive and eliminate the negative. It is an excellent teambuilding tool.

In the following chapters I outline some of the steps to increase Humour in the Workplace. The journey begins by recognizing there is great worth in mirth, and knowing that in our workplaces if we are not having fun – we are doing something wrong.

PEARL OF BIZDOM
2

IF YOU DON'T ASK, YOU DON'T GET

A networking opportunity, a newspaper article and a bit of nerve was all it took to get me to ask for something I really wanted. The positive answer changed the direction of my work.

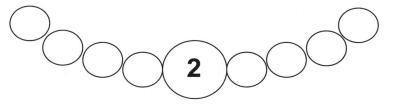

Just ask

Every Wednesday night, I go to Ladies Swim with my friend Lindsay. Well, every Wednesday that she can get the car, I'm not working, and our husbands can watch the kids. So maybe once a month.

Last week, as we were getting changed, I hadn't time for the obligatory "Does my bum look big in this?" I was bursting with news to share. I told her I had landed a monthly business column.

"Kate, that is fantastic, absolutely fantastic. Wow. **You** are going to be writing for the Business Section?" I wasn't sure what she was implying by the boldface type in her voice when she said 'You'. I decided to ignore it.

"It is fantastic isn't it?" I said.

"Absolutely fantastic, Kate."

"Yeah! Fantastic. " I made a mental note that if I was to write, I must learn more adjectives.

"But, Kate…"

"Yeah?"

"Don't you have to be a business expert?"

Crash, bang, boom. I hate that. Reality came crashing in, just when I was flying high in my own blue sky thinking.

"I may not have a degree," I protested, "But business isn't rocket science. And besides, I would make a great thumbnail photo."

I gave her my best impersonation of a business guru photo – serious, but earnest, hand casually touching chin.

She giggled.

We swam.

We paused for breath and a chat. Linz said, "Tell me more about this column, how did you get it?"

"I just asked."

"What? You just asked!?"

I was surprised by her surprise. It got me thinking. To me it's simple. When you see what you want, take the shortest path to get it – which is to just ask.

I told Lindsay about a recent networking dinner I attended. At my table was the editor of the local business paper. Not a thumbnail photo, but the 8" x 10" himself. I manoeuvred to sit next to him.

As we chatted during the soup, I was emboldened by two titbits I had read about success. First titbit: When Casanova was on his deathbed, friends and foes gathered round to hear his final words. "Cassy," they asked. "How is it you were so successful with all those women?" Legend has it that with his final smile and a sigh, he said, "I just asked."

Second titbit: A recent survey found that 75% of people who succeeded in getting a raise said "I just asked".

So as the main course was served, I turned to my dinner mate and I just asked. "Please may I write a business column for your paper?"

Needless to say the answer was yes.

Back at the pool, as I finished my story, Lindsay nodded and said, "Fantastic, but can I just ask... what if the answer was no?"

"Ah, Linz, if you want to succeed, "what if the answer is no?" is the only question you shouldn't ask."

Kate Hull Rodgers

PEARL OF BIZDOM
3

LAUGHTER IS THE BEST

In a business context, "Humourobics" is thinking outside the box. So far out, you end up saying "Box? What box?"

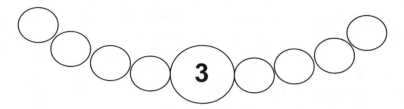

They who laugh, last

It was my dad, the career chiropractic, the drugless practitioner, who suggested I reclaim the phrase "Laughter is the best medicine." He pointed out that laughter is completely natural and truly there is nothing medical or man made about it.

Laughter is the best, but just how natural is it in our workplaces? For a decade and a half I have preached that laughter is the lynchpin to developing Humour in the Workplace. But it was not until 2003 that I began to see the British stiff upper lip begin to quiver.

I was invited to speak at a conference hosted by Business Link. The delegates represented companies who had achieved Investors in People status, companies who believed people to be their greatest asset.

I addressed the audience with a ream of statistics and evidence based research to prove that increasing humour would benefit their workplaces. I told of the measurable implications to increasing health - laughter can lower blood pressure, increase immunities, oxygenate the blood, aid digestion, burn calories and decrease treatment time.

One evaluation form came back reading, *"Kate, you needn't spend so much time convincing us of the merits of Humour in the Workplace. The fact that we are here today means we have bought your message. Just tell us what to do."*

Just tell us what to do!?! This was the green light I had been looking for. Please let this comment be more than just the tip of the iceberg. Please let it be that the entire British reserve was melting. Finally, I felt I could "hot up" my presentations.

I stopped spending so much time talking about the benefits of laughter. I began teaching people how to do it, so they could experience these benefits first hand. My session now included the anatomical reproduction of the physical act of laughter. This is an exercise that I call Humourobics.

Too often laughter in a workplace doesn't come naturally. Humourobics is a fun way to get our laughter muscles into shape. A bit like practicing scales on the piano so that one day we will be able to play jazz. Or it's like going to the gym and getting fit. If we then need to run for the bus, it is easier. By practicing Humourobics we laugh more readily when something amusing happens. And we are less likely to get stressed when we are challenged.

It doesn't matter what your personal sense of humour finds funny. Humourobics is laughter without reason. In today's stressed out, target driven world, if you wait for reasons to laugh, you just won't find enough of them. Instead, laugh first – on purpose – and you will start to find more things to laugh about. You will lighten up your perspective on things and find the lighter side. With Humourobics we do not laugh because we are

12

happy, we are happy because we laugh.

The exercise begins by simply putting a smile on your face. Not only does it feel good, but it also will start a bio-chemical response in your body; the release of natural endorphins. These are the body's feel good chemicals. They act as muscle relaxants and are a natural pain killer. They make us feel better. And what do we do when we feel better? We smile.

In other words we simulate laughter to stimulate laughter. We just fake it till we make it.

Laughter is the best, but sometimes we have to give it a helping hand. So we practice the discipline of Humourobics. We laugh till it helps.

PEARL OF BIZDOM
4

GOOD MANNERS MAKE GOOD BUSINESS

As soon as I could talk my parents taught me to say "please" and "thank you". It's an important lesson for business.

14

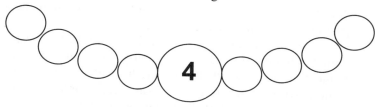

4

No time like the pleasant

My Mom called one Sunday when I badly needed her advice. I had messed up explaining the real meaning of Easter to my young son, Harvey. He concluded they call it Good Friday because Jesus was resurrected as the Easter Bunny.

Normally she would proffer some wise words but instead she was bursting to tell me about a driver who had cut her off in a parking lot.

"Kate, I had indicated I was going into the space. Even waved at the lady. And then she just revved it, and drove in the parking space. So rude. And she had three kids with her. What's that teaching them? Kate, you've plenty of time to sort my grandson about Easter, are you teaching him good manners!?!"

My mother has always been a font of knowledge, but since I've had kids of my own she seems even wiser. Once again, she was right to focus me on what is important. Good manners matter and we must pass them on, not just to our children, but to everyone.

A few days after my mother's rant, my husband Bill and I received a Miles Davis CD in the post. This was completely out of the blue. The unsigned card read, "Since you don't know this man's music, it's about time you were introduced." Bill and I instantly knew who it was from. The Chief Executive of Sheffield Theatres Limited, Grahame Morris.

I had been presenting some seminars in his theatre and we had talked about jazz music. I confessed I didn't know that much about it. And now through the post box came this unexpected gift.

I thought about how nice it was to do business with Grahame. He was a very busy man but always found time to be kind. Moreover, he was a successful leader. During his reign he was responsible for a complete turn around of the theatre's fortunes. Not only did he manage to keep the World Snooker competition in the venue, but his visionary leadership managed to entice Kenneth Brannagh back onto the stage after a 12 year hiatus. Brannagh could have played Richard III anywhere, but he chose Sheffield. Even in show business it is ultimately the business that shows.

'Please' and 'Thank you' cost nothing and yet will buy you almost anything. If you're a parent it's "the magic word", if you're a boy scout it's "a good deed a day", and if you're a Christian it's "the Golden Rule".

With Humour in the Workplace, there is a practice that encourages people to be nice to each other. It's called Acts of Kindness. It compliments good manners by actively giving staff members permission to do something nice for each other and seek no recompense.

The implementation can take on many forms. Many companies turn it into a weekly ritual. Each person chooses a colleague's name out of hat. They must commit an act of kindness for this person without revealing their identity. Employees will find a basket of fruit left on their desk or discover their car has been washed while they toiled at their desk. Companies often start a "Book of Kindnesses" where acts are recorded, making a testimonial worth celebrating.

One of the first clients I introduced these ideas to was Westfield, the contributory health service. They are a multi award winning company, have low staff turn over and excellent customer satisfaction records.

Employee well being is high on their agenda. I knew they would be receptive to Acts of Kindness.

During my speech at their annual conference I outlined how to implement the idea into their workplace. Then their Chief Executive, Graham Moore, told a story of his own. He recounted how he had become a kinder driver. One day, on the drive home, he approached a roundabout notorious for aggressive driving. He decided to let a few cars in. Traffic seemed to move more smoothly. He felt good doing good. That is until those cars let somebody else in! "Kindness is contagious!" he warned.

But then he told us when he got home, he checked his watch. He was very surprised to see that he had arrived 8 minutes faster than usual. He joked that kindness had transcended time.

Westfield continues to be a market leader.

Acts of Kindness can create many business opportunities. The sales and marketing manager of a Marriott Hotel attended a lunch at which I spoke. I had the delegates exchange business cards, with the instruction that they were to commit an Act of Kindness for the person whose card they got. The woman from the Marriott got the card of a training manager from Lloyds TSB. For her act of kindness, she invited the lady from the bank for a complimentary lunch at the hotel. The lunch went extremely well and in return Lloyds TSB booked their next training event for 150 delegates to be held at the hotel. That's nice business; that's good business.

Oh, and did I mention, Marriott Hotels and Lloyds TSB are now both clients of mine.

Simply decide where, when and for whom to commit Acts of Kindness. The main thing is to give without remembering, and to receive without forgetting.

After all, that's what our mothers taught us.

PEARL OF BIZDOM
5

QUIT YOUR JOB
EACH AND EVERY DAY

Too often work seems to follow us home. We need to leave it behind and get some balance.

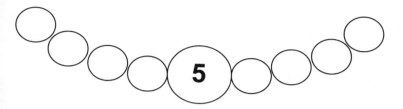

5

Switch off with a rite of passage

Yippee! It's a Bank Holiday weekend. In Canada we call it a Long Weekend. I think that's an oxymoron. Have you ever had a weekend that was long? They seem to be either short, too short, really short or so short you might just as well have stayed at the office. They seem to be – but are they really that short? I used to think so.

Despite the delicious anticipation of an extra day off, I never found time to lose myself in a good book. I'd have Monday night regrets; I hadn't gotten enough done and I'd only unwound enough to realize how tired I was. I'd 'banked' on the long weekend rejuvenating me and it hadn't.

Several of my clients have voiced similar concerns. They complain work infringes on their private time. With the advent of laptops, mobiles and blackberries it is now virtually impossible to lock their briefcases in the filing cabinet. Work seeps into life. More than ever before, we need to learn how to switch off work and switch on life.

One solution I now advocate is to develop a rite of passage. Develop a ritual that signifies the end of your workday and the beginning of the rest of your life. Separate work from life by marking the moment you clock off.

Your ritual should engage as many senses as possible; sound, sight, taste... but especially your sense of humour. The daily repetition of the ritual will gradually condition the mind and body to recognize the transition when we relax about work and rev up about life.

The passage can be done privately or with colleagues. Several of my clients have created their own fun, often outrageous, ways to mark the end of their workday.

A group of women who work on a complaint desk in a major retailer finish their day by closing and locking their office door. Then they stand in a circle and very slowly begin to beat their chests like Tarzan, with their "ah-a-ahs" growing louder and louder. Tension is replaced by laughter.

A call centre manager has a hand held mirror in her desk. She looks in the mirror and meows, signifying she no longer has to be the tiger.

A London architect decided that since his work was cerebral his passage would be surreal. To finish his workday he hops three times on his right foot, and four times on his left.

Sound silly? So it should. During work our behaviour is logical, often predictable. The passage provides a momentary halt, a gear shift, so we can regroup. We literally change our skin. After all, most people change their clothes when they finish work. This is the exact same idea now taken further.

Clients who develop these rituals report a feeling of release, relaxation and yes, silliness. Most importantly they report a perceptible marking of the end of work. It is important to consciously register the uplifting feeling of "I am off duty".

Clients report that being truly 'switched off' work allows them to rejuvenate more quickly. They can return to work the next day with renewed vim and vigour.

I've been practicing for over a year now, and I know this bank holiday weekend actually will be a long, long weekend. I have fully switched off from work.

Now where was that "chick lit" book I was reading...?

PEARL OF BIZDOM
6

SUCCESS IS SUBJECTIVE

We can't all be prodigies or geniuses. Sometimes just being ordinary is excellent.

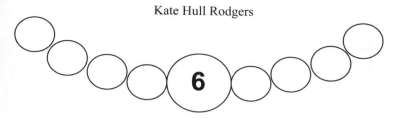

Tumbling to real success

"You are living in mediocrity." Ouch. Coming from my father, this judgment really hurt. I was speechless, I had no reply.

It happened during a call home to Canada. As usual, I tried to impress my father. In this case, my attempt was definitely misguided. I gushed to him about my new life in northern England. I espoused the friendliness of Yorkshire folk. "They are so down to earth, Dad, they think nothing of having their knickers drying on the radiator." My father was appalled. Thus the proclamation about me and mediocrity.

Turns out Dad was not offended because unmentionables were on show. Rather, he was dismayed that my husband Bill and I didn't have a dryer. Dad's definition of success, it seems, is directly related to ownership of major appliances.

I relayed the story to Bill's 92-year-old Granny. Clara is Yorkshire born and bred, and has been through 2 world wars. She too was dismayed; not because of my father's value system, but for a very different reason. "You mean to tell me that Canadians have tumble dryers – in the house!?"

To my father, the absence of a dryer meant mediocrity. To Granny, the presence of a dryer was sheer decadence. Growing up on different continents during different eras, they have very different measures of success.

Success is subjective. It is determined by age, sex, religion, homeland, family, and contemporary must haves. Success is highly personal and changes as we change.

I came of age in the 80s, when success seemed tangible. Success was a target you could drive toward. Big house, big car, big family, big bank balance. I drove so hard toward the land of big that I went round the bend.

During my twenties, I tried to be the newly-liberated, educated, Generation X Superwoman. I wanted the ultimate career, the perfect man, the adorable babies. I wanted more, more, more – except cellulite on my thighs, of course. No matter what I accomplished I still hadn't found what I was looking for and I couldn't get no satisfaction.

It was enough to drive anyone mad. And that's exactly what happened to me. The only thing I gained was weight and the only thing I lost was my mind. I had a nervous breakdown. I was hospitalized in a mental institution for over a year.

During this time, I began to realize that much of my unhappiness came from measuring success by someone else's yardstick. Breaking down gave me the opportunity to put myself back together – better than ever.

I determined I wanted to discover my own definition of success. I knew success wasn't just about being bigger and having more.

Eventually, I discharged myself from hospital. My psychiatrist didn't think I was ready, but he couldn't detain me. On my exit papers he declared me a disabled adult. The prognosis he gave me included the declaration "Kate will never have meaningful work." But I have had the last laugh, I became a business consultant. Having a nervous breakdown turned out to be the best career move I ever made.

On my quest to understand the meaning of success I have worked with organizations around the world. I have observed that many businesses that appear outwardly 'successful' are peopled by staff who feel inwardly empty. Too often the business is bigger but the people have become smaller.

Just after my call with my Dad and my chat with Granny, I had a consultation with a client whom I asked to define success in his business. "We set targets, we achieve them. That's success." "And then what?" I asked. "Then we set higher targets, we achieve those." He paused and he thought. "After awhile," he admitted "I can't help but wonder, what's the point? Is this as good as it gets?"

I begin to see that success is not a destination. It is a journey. Bill Marriott Junior, head of the $15 billion global business that bears his name, surely understands success. He says "There is no finish line, no ultimate summit, no having it all."

If the journey is to be a successful one, there must be times when we stop striving and start arriving. There must be times when we aren't driving toward bigger, or trying to achieve a target. We need to work as if we don't need a new dryer.

When climbing the corporate ladder we mustn't be afraid to look down and celebrate how far we have come.

Hitting rock bottom was in many ways more enriching than reaching the top. But I don't wish to relive my twenties. However, I do wish I could have the telephone conversation with my Dad to do over again. How I wish I could have calmly said, "Mediocrity? You know, Dad, sometimes mediocre is okay."

PEARL OF BIZDOM
7

TAKE TIME, MAKE TIME

There never seems to be a good time for a break.
There will always be something left undone.

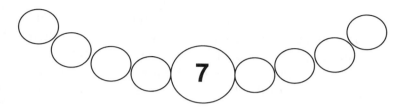

The panic before the calm

I haven't got time to write this. I'm going on holiday next week. Can't wait to be jetting off to see friends and family in Canada. Just me and my little boys, Harvey and Dominic. My big boy, Bill, has some acting work and won't be joining us. We thought of changing our holiday time, but it's been ages since I had a break and the boys are growing so fast my family won't know them.

Is there ever a good time to take a holiday? All this week I've been in a panic. I've emails to reply to, reports to submit, accounts to calculate, phone calls to make, clothes to pack, game boys to charge and this chapter to write.

I am not alone in this challenge to take a break. Last year, one in five workers in the UK did not take all their paid leave. One in 10 worked all year without taking any time off at all. Two out of three people admitted to never taking a proper lunch break, and half of our workforces are doing regular unpaid overtime. Goodwill they call it.

No wonder stress has over taken the common cold as the number one reason for workplace absenteeism. No wonder the Health and

Safety Executive has placed stress as one of its top 6 priorities.

I begin to wonder - why is it managers will send their staff home and then burn the midnight oil? Doctors prescribe as they cough into their hankie? And teachers tell their classes to calm down yet they have the highest stress levels of any profession. And why is this the first holiday I've taken in years?

I haven't got time to wonder why; I've got to get this chapter written. I really can't afford the time off work. It's such a busy time. I have so much to do to get ready, so many things to tie up.

But my mind begins to wonder... I imagine myself on the airplane, listening attentively to the air stewardess point out the escape routes. This holiday is my escape. I can imagine the stewardess looking pointedly at me, then at my boys. I can hear her saying "If you are travelling with small children, place the oxygen mask over your own face first..." This snaps me out of my reverie. First? Place the oxygen mask over my face first? That goes against every parenting instinct. I wouldn't look after myself first; I would look after my children first.

And then the penny drops. The airline's safety precautions make sense. If I don't take care of myself, I won't be able to do my job. Whether it's looking after the kids or looking after the business, it is a matter of survival.

I still haven't got time to write this. I still haven't got time for a holiday. But I must take one, I must make time. I must refill myself so that I can give from a full cup.

And so now I confess I've decided to leave emails unanswered, invoices uncollected, accounts uncalculated and this chapter unfini......

PEARL OF BIZDOM
8

MODERATION IN DELEGATION

Behind many new good ideas there lurk some very bad outcomes.

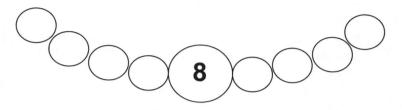

Outsourcing the laundry

My washing machine broke this week. No panic, I outsourced the laundry. Thank goodness there's a nearby drop-it-off-dirty-pick-it-up-clean Laundromat.

The VAT is due and all the receipts are in a shoe box. No worries, I outsourced it. Thank goodness my bookkeeper can balance my books while I balance my work life.

It's school holidays and the children need minding. No problem, I outsourced it. Thank goodness for Working Family Tax Credit and Ofsted or there might not be four, count 'em, four, resourceful, qualified, trustworthy childminders I use. And that's just on a Wednesday.

Outsourcing is all the rage. It is defined as "hiring an individual or organization to take over and become responsible for tasks traditionally handled by internal staff". I love outsourcing. It has relieved me of much guilt. I no longer feel bad for farming out my children, instead I feel glad for having made a strategic business choice to outsource their care. Yes, that feels better. Honest.

Outsourcing is said to increase efficiency and decrease expenses. It is easy to decide if outsourcing is financially a good idea. Simply figure your hourly worth, and then calculate how long it takes you to do certain tasks. Measure this against how much it would cost to outsource those tasks. For instance, if my time is worth £50 per hour, and it takes me an hour and a half (or £75) to prepare Sunday tea, it would be a financially intelligent choice to outsource this task to the grocery store. It takes me just over half an hour to travel to the shop and buy their precooked chicken, ready made roasties and salad in a bag and travel back. I've saved the equivalent of about £48. Fantastic. I'll never cook again.

If my time is worth £50 per hour and my book keeper charges £15, and does it faster… you see the logic.

Manufacturing giants like Sony see the logic too. They have outsourced part of their electronics production to Solectron Corporation in California, and PlayStation production has gone to mainland China. Even British Telecom has begun to outsource its call centres.

This makes me pause for thought. The telephone company is outsourcing its telephone calls?!? Outsourcing needs more scrutiny.

To outsource seems to make perfect financial sense when you compare hourly rates. But are there some unforeseen repercussions? The answer is yes.

Recent research has found increased stress levels in companies that are outsourcing and using contracted services. Anxiety levels are high as workers wait for the outsourcing monster to gobble up their jobs. Absenteeism is on the increase.

The backlash from employees has manifested in another measurable way. There is a marked rise in turnover of key staff. Even if they are assured their jobs are safe, valued employees are increasingly becoming pre-emptive in determining their future. It always looks and feels better to have left a job voluntarily. And so the new lean, mean, corporate machine is left sputtering.

Off-shore outsourcing has become a contentious social/economic/labour issue. Companies that have chosen to use out of country staff are now having customer service surveys which are often negative.

Outsourcing at first glance seems a great idea, but should be practiced with discernment. The backlash has begun and there is already a newer, must-do idea. It is called Re-Insourcing. Jargon for "do it yourself."

Guess I'd better get the washer fixed, but I'll stick with the book keeper. And I'll rethink the four childminders in one day. After all I don't want my kids to start calling me Aunt Kate.

PEARL OF BIZDOM
9

THE ONLY CONSTANT IS CHANGE

Change is like most workplace challenges; it all depends on how you look at it.

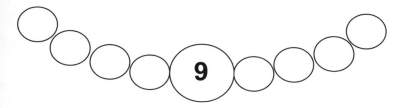

9

The I of the Storm

'There is no I in TEAM'. This was written in bold print, on a plaque on the wall behind my client's head. I was there to discuss her upcoming conference. I had been asked to speak about change. So what else is new? Change management is now old hat. No wonder my mind was wandering and my eyes landed on the sign: There is no I in TEAM.

Some clever business guru had coined this phrase. But I like to question the writing on the wall. I decided it was wrong. A team is made up of I's. The stronger the I's the stronger the team. The expected sacrifice of individualism is at the root of much unhappiness in the modern workplace.

Staring at that clever little sign I began to imagine that even the word TEAM was made up of many I's. The letter T is made up of two I's, one stands tall, propping the second one across its top. The letter A is three I's, two leaning against each other, the third connecting them lower down.

A voice brought me back to the meeting room. It was my client. "So with all this happening," she said, "We knew the conference had to focus on change. Organizational change. What shall we call your session Kate?"

Change? I had been focusing on TEAM. "I... I... I..." I stumbled. And then out popped "I of the Storm". Let's call the session "I of the Storm".

Change is a huge issue, and a familiar one. Alvin Toffler coined the phrase *future shock* in 1970, which now seems like ancient history. Future shock: "the shattering stress and disorientation that we induce in individuals by subjecting them to too much change in too short a time." This, I believe, outlines the challenge; to implement organizational change without shattering the individual.

In business, changes are often made to prepare for the future. This can cause discord. Some staff will feel the changes are thrust upon them, they may see the future challenges differently than management does. As the Chinese proverb says; "To prophesy is extremely difficult – especially with respect to the future." Too often change feels like change for change sake. But if a company is to keep ahead, innovation and change must be constant.

Toffler predicted that unless we learn to control the rate of change, we are doomed. But we can't stop change, nor can we control its rate, as Toffler advised. What we can do, however, is choose how we respond to it. We don't have to be shocked. We can avoid the stress.

We can think of change as a whirlwind; fast moving, perhaps wreaking havoc in its path. Then we can minimize any negative effects if we remember that at the centre of every tornado is a point of peace, a calm stillness. That point is the eye of the storm, the 'I'. If change does not threaten the "I", the change will not be as disorienting. The ideal team will respect the individual and their core values. A strong organization can manage change without the sacrifice of individualism.

I see a similar theme in David Bowie's classic song "Changes". He urges us to "turn and face the strain", and observes "I watch the ripples change their size but never leave the stream." This describes, I believe, the constancy within change.

It is time for the writing on the wall to change. The plaques should now read: "The whole is greater that the sum of its parts".

Or, on a lighter note; "Change is inevitable, except from a vending machine."

PEARL OF BIZDOM
10

FLIRT WITH SUCCESS

*Children shouldn't play with matches, should adults
play with fire?*

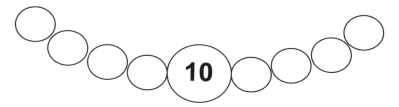

Bring back banter

Virtual foreplay, window shopping, European charm, or attention without intention. It's called flirting, and it's made a comeback. I think we have Penelope Cruz to thank. At the height of her popularity, she had already won the hearts of Matt Damon, Russell Crowe, Nicolas Cage and was dating Tom Cruise. She was asked about her secret to success with men. She batted her black Spanish eyelashes and replied to the reporter, "Well," bat, bat, "I like to flirt." Her 'secret to success' made headlines.

Suddenly daytime TV devoted entire programs to flirting, featuring a new breed of experts; flirt coaches. Glittery t-shirts proclaimed FLIRT, how-to flirt books became best sellers.

I became involved in the movement when SpiceUK, the adult social club, asked me to develop a flirting seminar for their members. The session I created taught how to build rapport, read body language, and enjoy complimenting. We called it Flirting for Fun. When it was offered to Spice members, each session sold out faster than a Madonna concert.

Clearly there was a demand for flirting skills in social situations. I began to realize there could be a crossover into the realm of business. The skills of flirting are the exact same skills required when we are networking, building relationships or communicating.

Penelope and Tom have long since parted company but flirting is here to stay. I think it's time for British business to bring back banter.

A few decades ago, workplaces became politically correct, and banter was virtually banned. This change was celebrated by women, striving for equal opportunity without the 'teasing' harassment.

But it's time to evolve again. There is now a case for loosening up. If we have become equals in our workplaces, then there's a lot of opportunity for grown-up playfulness without offence. The game is called flirting. The rules are quite clear – this is attention without intention. It's about seduction, teasing, innuendo, complimenting and relationship building. Ultimately it's about the joy of the chase, not the catch.

Flirting in business is definitely increasing in popularity. A recent survey by New Woman Magazine found that 8 out of 10 women like to flirt at work. The revival makes sense because the object of flirting is simple: You make your flirting partner feel good and they make you feel good. The relationship is mutual and reciprocal. We all want to do business with the colleague, client or customer who makes us feel good.

Flirting relies on the willingness to add a little spice to encounters, to allow ambiguity, suspense, intrigue, and subtlety. You have to want to play, and trust the other players. You share the understanding that anyone can quit at anytime without repercussions. Flirting is based on trust; this is why it can help the walls between people come tumbling down. The relationships formed can go from formal to friendship to flirting. Flirting is undoubtedly an under-used tool in teambuilding, customer care and workplace communication.

Compliments are the currency of a good flirting session. Even the vocabulary is one of business, you "pay" compliments and you reap many rewards.

The rapport flirting builds can be so powerful it heightens all the senses. This sensuality leads to better perceptive abilities. It helps us to become sensitive to body language, and to interpret non verbal signals more accurately. We communicate better.

All these benefits far outweigh the possible pitfalls. Yes, of course, there are pitfalls. Intention does not always equal interpretation. But misunderstanding is a possibility in all forms of communication. True flirting occurs in an atmosphere of equality, and when both people want to play. If flirting or teasing is about exercising power, or putting your own needs above others, then it falls into the realm of harassment. The goal of flirting is making your flirt partner happy, not uncomfortable.

Trust yourself, have the confidence to act as your instincts direct, and you will discover your unique flirting techniques. Have fun, and always respect the golden rule: Do unto your flirt partners, as you would have them do unto you.

Politically correct doesn't have to mean boring and the loss of charm. In my house, PC means Parental Control.

So hey, all you gorgeous smart people...Let's put some spice in our business. Let's bring back banter.

PEARL OF BIZDOM
11

COMPETE

But remember, winning isn't everything.

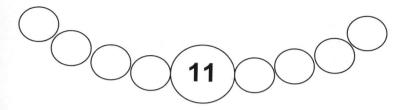

11

My happy villain

I've been living with the Villain of the Year. Or at least one of the nominees. Yes, my dear sweet husband is up for a British Soap Award for Villain of the Year. He's off to walk the red carpet with all the other luminaries. He's grinning like a Cheshire cat.

Will Bill win and be named Britain's biggest baddie? The media have all said he should, but I say he won't. No, I'm not an unsupportive wife, I'm a realist. The playing field isn't level.

The British Soap Award for Villain of the Year is won through a phone-in vote. Bill appeared as Evil Eddie in just 13 episodes of a daytime soap, Doctors. It only has a fraction of the viewing audiences of the night time soaps. He simply can't compete with the likes of villains from Coronation Street or East Enders who enter our living rooms 4 times a week for months, if not years. The press may be right, Bill should win on merit. But on the night it will be about numbers. And they just don't add up in Bill's favour.

So why is he smiling? I certainly wasn't smiling when I didn't win Start Up of the Year at our local business awards. I was so cross when a huge company won that I've not entered a competition since. I was so cross because the playing field wasn't level. What does Bill know that I don't?

"Well, Kate," he said, "You are very competitive but you don't know how to compete."

What on earth is that supposed to mean? He continued, "Don't you remember what you said to Harvey when he didn't win at sports day? What do all mothers say to their children?"

And the penny dropped. (For those of you who have never been children, I'll tell you what all mothers say to their children: "Honey, it's not whether you win or lose, it's how you play the game. It's taking part that matters.") I said this to my son, and what's more, I believed it.

Why then, when it comes to business, do I think only winning counts? Maybe because this idea is reinforced everywhere. Just this week I've heard of three corporate seminars - Natural Born Winners, Playing to Win, and Leading Winners.

When I look at Bill's smile I see the rewards of taking part are as good as the award itself. For this villainous nomination, his rewards include reading the complimentary media about himself, walking the red carpet, networking at the show biz party, the subsequent pub stories he'll have to tell, having 'nominee' on his CV, buying a new bow tie, and knowing his mother would be proud; proud that he's taking part.

Bill reminds me that when I didn't win the Start Up award, I did more than stamp my feet. I also did a perspective check on what I really want.

It's not that I can't compete with big business; it's that I don't want to. I want a flexible lifestyle and worklife balance. I want to go swimming at off-peak times, I want to let the phone ring when Doctors is on, and mostly I want to attend my kid's sports day.

I now realize that winners win, which is good; but I also see that losers learn, which is sometimes even better.

I've got to go; Bill's asked me to record the award ceremony. Fingers crossed…

PEARL OF BIZDOM
12

HYDRATE, HYDRATE, HYDRATE

When we get dehydrated we get stressed, and when we get stressed we get dehydrated.

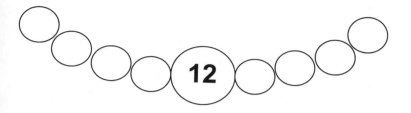

12

The crystal clear water of life

Water is the essence of life. When the young, deaf, dumb and blind Helen Keller communicated her famous first word, the word was WATER. When Quasimodo, the hunchback of Notre Dame, expressed his love for Esmeralda he marvelled; "You gave me water." It was a poetic metaphor for "You gave me life."

Never underestimate the power of water. Drinking water will increase your attention span, memory, productivity, and general sense of well-being and health.

In our bodies, water accounts for 92% of the blood, 75% of the brain, 75% of the muscles and 22% of the bones. Therefore, even moderate dehydration can cause headaches, dizziness, achy joints, stiffness and fatigue. Medical research has linked reduced water intake to asthma, allergies, arthritis, angina, hypertension, high cholesterol, chronic fatigue, multiple sclerosis, depression and diabetes.

Continuous hydration is recommended. Experts now recognize that by the time we are thirsty, it's too late. The negative effects of dehydration have already begun.

To avoid dehydration experts suggest we measure our body weight in pounds and then drink half that amount in ounces. In other words, if you weigh 140 pounds, you should drink 70 ounces of water. Building up intake gradually will allow the body to adjust.

Making water available in a workplace is easy. There is no need for planning, policy making, consultants or new computer programs. The required budget is minimal.

An effective implementation is to introduce a hydration awareness program. Not only must we lead people to the water, but we must encourage them to drink.

The education system has long recognized the positive affects of drinking water. Paula Harmer was one of the first head teachers in the UK to implement a hydration awareness program for her staff and students.

"We began by educating the children on the benefits of drinking water. Then each child was designated their own water bottle which they decorated to create a sense of ownership. They bring water from home; this involves the parents and encourages drinking water to become part of family life. The children keep their bottles at their desk and self-regulate their intake. No longer is water a quick drink at a fountain, it is an integral part of our day." Paula reports a particular improvement in concentrations levels in the afternoon.

Research shows that the placement of a water cooler will greatly effect how much water is drunk. If an employee must pass the desk of a superior, they are less likely to visit the cooler. If the cooler becomes a centre of networking, more water is drunk. As with the children, there is an increase in intake if people use their own water bottles and are able to have them at their work stations. The least effective containers in encouraging water consumption are disposable cups.

There's more to water than just drinking. The benefits of seeing and hearing water are well researched in corporate America. One study 'The Role of Nature in Human Well Being and Workplace Development' revealed; "Employees with views of water report fewer headaches, less job pressure and greater job satisfaction." If lakeside offices are in short supply at your workplace, rest assured; photographs of water reportedly work almost as well. Companies and health clinics have begun to replace music with the sound of running water. Reception areas are featuring plasma screens playing footage of waterfalls, rivers and rhythmic ocean waves.

It's crystal clear; hydrate your workplace.

PEARL OF BIZDOM
13

DON'T TRY TO DO IT ALL

Ever start to achieve everything you ever wanted, only to discover you can't remember why you wanted it in the first place?

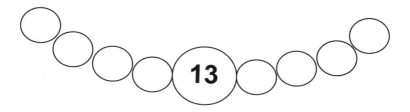

13

Juggle Struggle takes its toll

She was tall, slim, and drop dead gorgeous. Her cryptic Mona Lisa smile held a thousand secrets, and her left hand held a Virginia Slim cigarette. She was the woman's answer to the Marlboro Man. The advertisers proclaimed to 70s North American women "You've come a long way, baby." Little wonder I had my first smoke at 9.

Having come this supposed long way; I can't help wondering where, as a woman, I am. I examine a day in my life. The morning begins with me on the computer doing yesterday's work. My husband feeds and dresses our kids. He takes them to the childminder. Together they are the mothers of my children. I'm not there.

I read the Business Year in Review in my local paper. Pictures speak the loudest, and shouting from the newspaper pages are photos of men, men, men and more men. I'm not there.

Here I am, doing a Wonder Woman twirl, donning my new power suit. It's EntreprenHer, up, up and away!

I'm off to network at a business woman's lunch, where the speaker is one the few female University Vice Chancellors in the UK. I find myself surrounded by women who have come a long way.

During the luncheon I enthuse about the newest member of the HumourUs team, Vickie. I tell that she has been hired to help us increase our operational effectiveness. Then I confess she also does light housework, picks up groceries and straightens my collar. "Her job title would be 'Wife'" I joke, "Except that I pay her." We all laugh, but I'm not sure why.

The speech is a well-researched look at how far we have come, baby, in the world of higher education. It's a world perceived as being liberal, open minded and equal in opportunity. But the statistics don't bear this out. Women in high places are few and far between, the highest female salary is only one third that of the male counterpart, and there are very few female Fellows. No pun intended.

The discussion afterwards is lively. Girls schools are superior – shame I can't send my sons. Women are often held back by other women – misogyny sometimes wears a skirt. Women can get job satisfaction without the big salary – oh no they can't, equal pay for equal work, oh yes they can, a good job is reward enough…

My head begins to swim. I'm not sure where I sit on any of these discussion points. I make my excuses – I've got to get to the bank before the school run – and leave.

At the bank, there are 57 tellers standing in a row – all women, and 3 suited managers seated at their desks – all men.

I hurry past the newsagents and see that there are photos of women on nearly every front page. There they are, in the top right hand corner; young, blonde, with store-bought boobs and botoxed butts. But it's a long way, baby, to get a photo in the business pages.

By evening I am exhausted. The Juggle Struggle of modern woman takes its toll. Wife, mother, boss, peer. Who am I? I am all. And that is what I want, I want it all. I want my kids to run to me when they fall down. I want to be tall, slim and drop dead gorgeous. I want to make bags of money. I want to go out on a date with my husband and not discuss our business. Mostly, I want to feel I have come a long way.

But I don't. Instead, as I fall asleep, I feel overwhelmed. I don't feel that I have come a long way. Striving for it all sometimes makes me feel like I have been running in circles.

PEARL OF BIZDOM
14

TELLING A JOKE IS A SERIOUS BUSINESS

If we don't want a punch line to cause a punch up, then we must examine how and why we tell jokes in a workplace.

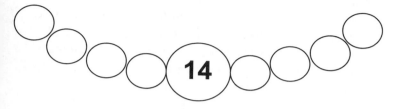

Joking aside?

Jokes are a good place to start when implementing Humour in the Workplace. They are a great communication tool and build rapport in relationships.

But jokes often run the risk of offending someone, so it's best to have a strategy. Sad, yes, to have a strategy for sharing jokes – but necessary if jokes are to be allowed and encouraged.

As a general rule, jokes in the workplace should not be gratuitous. Save those jokes for the pub. Workplace jokes are most beneficial when they make a point. Like a court jester to a king, much can be said through humour.

For example, a financial consultant uses a joke to explain how a business disaster like Enron might occur; "Old MacDonald had a farm and on this farm he had a donkey; but the donkey died. The farmer had invested in buying the donkey; how would he ever get his money back, let alone turn a profit? He decided to sell the donkey. How could he sell a dead donkey? He raffled it. He sold 500 tickets at £2 a pop. That's a £1000 for a dead donkey that would have sold for £250 alive. It wasn't until the prize was drawn that anyone discovered the donkey was dead. There was only one complaint – from the guy who won. So Old McDonald gave him back his two quid. E e i e i o!"

This is a classic punch line joke that quickly makes a point, brings laughter and opens listeners to hearing more about the subject matter.

One key to telling jokes is delivery. Often it is not what you say; it's how you say it. An important element to delivery is timing. Mastering timing has to do with the speed of delivery and the use of pauses. To 'play the pause' is to stop speaking in order to create focus and suspense. It gives the delivery rhythm and can subconsciously signal to the listener that the laughter point is coming.

Often it is fear of foolishness that stops many a potential humourist. So great is this fear that we use the expression, "I was so embarrassed I thought I would die." We equate being laughed at with death. Overcoming this can be simple; laugh at yourself first. With a deft touch you can poke a little fun at yourself. That way, anyone else who laughs is laughing with you.

Another method of introducing humour is to share a funny story. Stories allow audiences to laugh, chuckle, and smile throughout the telling. The humour is not reliant on people "getting it". There is opportunity to shape the story depending on the reactions of the listeners.

Recently at a business awards dinner, I shared the speaking platform with a Managing Director of a large company. Her use of humour was exemplary. She warmed up the audience with a story of her youthful misadventure at an event similar to the one we were attending. In her story, the venue was under construction and she fell headlong into a deep ditch. She had us laughing as she regaled us with her attempts to get out, her head barely reaching ground level, her dress ruined and hiked up. Finally she was pulled out, muddy and dishevelled. Then she finished her story by declaring "In life, as in business - what goes down will always come up".

Her nobody's perfect approach served to humanize her expertise and the moral of the story became the teaching point of her speech.

The strategic use of jokes and funny stories in the workplace will improve communication and relationships.

A good joke teller will practice, and joke telling is a practice that is good.

PEARL OF BIZDOM
15

MAKE THE DREAM FIT YOU

Don't set yourself up for failure. Sometimes it's best just to move the goal posts closer.

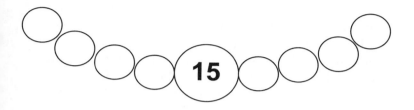

From classical failure to rock chick

This year I have made the best New Year's resolution ever. I have resolved to never make another New Year's resolution. Never, ever.

This decision is radical for a girl like me hooked on self-improvement.

Last year I resolved not to resolve something I had resolved before. If I had not accomplished the resolution in a year, then maybe I never really wanted to do it in the first place. So for the first time in 27 years, yes 27 years, last year's resolution was not "I will master the classical guitar". I had resolved this so many times it had become a bit of an obsession.

Each January, I would bring out my nylon string guitar and try, try, try. I have no natural musical ability and it was like banging my head against a wall. By mid February the guitar would be returned to its case, and I would feel dejected.

The obsession to improve myself by learning guitar was born of advice I received from an influential consultant - my high school principal.

At a parent-teacher meeting, not dissimilar to a quarterly appraisal, he began by citing my accomplishments. They were many, I was a scholastic over-achiever. Then he moved on to the changes that "had to be made." The Principal, (read 'Chief Executive'), spoke not to me, but to my parents (read 'on-line managers'). "Things come too easily for Kate. An unchallenged child is an unfulfilled adult." He told my parents to "push her to do something she isn't good at".

As a stress management consultant, I often see this played out in the workplace.

"Why are you stressed?"

"I'm not properly equipped for this job."

"Then why are you doing it?"

"My manager thought it would stretch me."

Yes, probably to the breaking point. This pushing of ourselves isn't just challenging us; sometimes it is setting ourselves up for failure.

I spent 27 long years trying to learn to play classical guitar, and I haven't got a musical bone in my body. I sounded like a metronome in a submarine. It never made me happy. So last year I quit trying. I resolved to work to my strengths, not highlight my weaknesses.

I began advising clients to do the same; "If you aren't succeeding, stop doing it." It sounded good, but somehow I knew there was more to this lesson than just accepting limitations.

The next revelation took place the following Christmas. My husband gave me an electrical guitar and amp. I looked at him in dismay, and dare I say, anger.

"Bill, you know I don't want to learn guitar!!!! I've tried so many times."

"Exactly."

"Exactly what!?"

He smiled the cryptic smile of a man who can play nine instruments by ear. "Stop trying," he said, "Just play."

So I've turned the amp up to a Spinal Tap 11 and rather than mastering the instrument, I'm making noise. It's a lot of fun, and it's beginning to sound like music. My music.

My advice to clients now is "If at first you don't succeed, try, try, try it different."

New Year's resolutions by their very nature deem that we want to be something or someone else. This year I've recognized that if I embrace the person I am, rather than reach to be someone I'm not, I will actually accomplish more. I just have to find my way of doing it.

I've learned that I couldn't master classical guitar, but I could still become a rock chick. Rather than bang my head against the wall, I've become a head banger. Instead of resolving to change me, I changed the dream.

PEARL OF BIZDOM
16

GO AHEAD, TOUCH SOMEONE

The handshake is the beginning and end of many a business encounter. Make it count.

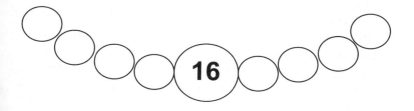

16

Putting the squeeze on a relationship

Let's get practical. Let's make your handshake count. The handshake is one of the few acceptable touches in British business. Used properly it is a fantastic builder of rapport. And don't underestimate the importance of the subliminal or covert messages you send.

We've all been told the firm handshake is best; the wet fish is a no-no. As a guideline, that'll do. But we live in an age where you can download 4 billion ringtones when a simple 'b-rrrrring b-rrrrring' would do. It's time to get sophisticated and really work that 'shake.

Your handshake should be memorable and signature. Practice, play and improvise till you find several that work. Focusing on your handshake may make you self conscious, but with time it becomes more natural.

A handshake can be formal, friendly or familiar. With practice, you will be able to modulate your approach depending on whose hand you are shaking and when.

To experiment, try these tips.

The Quick Squeeze – Shake hands, then finish the handshake with a tiny extra squeeze. It's like a physical wink; it's conspiratorial, just between you and me. It creates a sense of sincerity to your salutations. "It was great to see you again," shake, shake, "Hope it won't be so long next time," squeeze.

The Double Touch – When you are shaking with the right hand, don't forget the left. Using your left hand to touch opens many possibilities. You could brush the top of their hand, a quick touch. Or you could do a sustained touch with both your hands; it is almost like holding the other person's hand. It can be very reassuring and welcoming. The double touch can be on their forearm. This sends a signal of strength and warmth. Beware of getting too near their elbow, it feels like you want to escort them back to their nursing home. There is great scope to touching someone on the left shoulder whilst shaking their right hand. This is like a pat on the back.

Having mastered the permissible touch of handshaking, there is potential to explore other greetings that use touching.

The Kiss – This is a regular greeting in continental Europe, but is slow to make it to the shores of Britain. Perhaps it is because we never know if it is one cheek or two... do you kiss their cheek or just brush the air? Much of that is a matter of taste. But what is a matter of fact; kissing is a vastly underused rapport builder in Britain.

It is excellent to develop a relationship by greeting an associate with the classic firm handshake, then leaving them with a kiss. This signifies you have had a productive encounter. Formal at the start, familiar at the end.

To successfully offer a kiss, it is best to first gain permission. No, this doesn't mean you ask directly. You begin with an acceptable touch - shake their hand. Then, rather than letting go, you keep hold. Gently pull them toward you. This is the moment you should be reading their body language. If they follow your lead and lean toward you, get in there and kiss their right cheek. Done. If you feel any resistance, then let go. Don't force a kiss.

If a firm handshake is all you've got, perhaps you should think about "downloading" some new touch options.

PEARL OF BIZDOM
17

SEARCH FOR THE HERO
INSIDE AND OUT

It is important to know who you admire and who admires you.

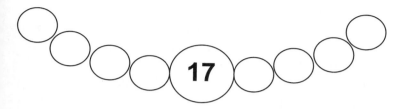

17

Of heroes, gurus and mentors

The call came. "Kate, can you speak as a Role Model?"

The letter arrived. "Who would you nominate as an inspirational Woman in Business?"

The magazine printed. "Special Issue celebrates European Heroes."

The corporate video played. "You've got to search for the Hero inside yourself…"

Everywhere I turn, the world seems obsessed with heroes, role models, mentors, gurus.

And yet, the more I've been asked to speak, nominate or search, the more I realize I don't know who my heroes are.

The call was to speak as a role model for entrepreneurs. A role model!?! Me? I had never thought of myself in that way.

But, if an entrepreneur by definition is someone who creates wealth from nothing, I qualify. I have always created my own opportunities. And apparently, I am a new breed; I am a lifestyle entrepreneur. It sounds terribly romantic, but actually means no one pays into my pension but me. So yes I am a happy entrepreneur, but I had no idea this meant I might be a Role Model to others. I feel honoured.

The letter asked me to nominate an Inspirational Woman in Business. Many women came to mind but finally, I chose author J.K. Rowling. I did not choose her because of her successful books, movies and merchandize. I nominated her because of her timing. She had the idea for Harry Potter long before she actually wrote the first book. But she waited until her daughter started school before she sat down with a laptop. To me she embodies the importance of knowing your priorities and keeping business in perspective. I feel inspired.

The magazine I read was Time. The cover story is about the results of a reader vote on Europe's Greatest Heroes. Both Tony Blair and Jacques Chirac made the short list. I find this very interesting because their nominations have to do with the War in Iraq. As they stood on opposite sides about waging that war, I could only conclude that one person's hero is another person's fool. I am always amazed when I learn that other people see things completely differently than I see them. I feel enlightened.

The video was from ACME PLC. I speak at a lot of big conferences, where invariably, the Chief Exec makes a speech about how different we are, then plays the same video I saw at last week's 'unique' event. If it isn't Tina Turner assuring me that I am simply the best, then it's Heather Small asking me what I've done to make me proud. I can't miss the irony in the fact that as we strive to be different we are all actually the same. The songs may be cliché but the desire is archetypal. I feel connected.

Instinctively we need heroes. They personify what makes us proud, what is the best. I'm glad I was called and written to. It has prompted me to identify who my gurus are and who I might be inspiring.

Personal success can be measured as you move from mentee to mentor, from worshipper to guru. I believe this movement is circular, like links in a chain. My guru may be learning from someone I have taught. Knowing my heroes and being a hero has made me feel part of a collective consciousness. I feel whole.

Kate Hull Rodgers

PEARL OF BIZDOM
18

READ MORE CHILDREN'S BOOKS

Good stories will always have a moral, an allegory, or a metaphor. There is much to learn.

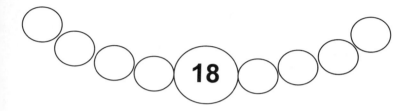

18

License to chill in wonderland

"I'm late, I'm late
For a very important date.
No time to say hello, goodbye
I'm late, I'm late, I'm late."

We all know the words, we all know the image. Lewis Carroll's White Rabbit is in many ways as prophetic a character as George Orwell's Big Brother. The stressed out self-important bunny is so busy going places that he doesn't know where he is. In the modern workplace his waistcoat has become a suit and tie, his pocket watch is now a blackberry.

Rush, rush, rush. We've all seen these busy bunnies. The colleague who's gotta go, can't talk, back-to-back meetings, emails up to the eyeballs, reports to file, proposals to make. Their illusion of power is fed by the Alices of the world. Alices believe if he's so busy, he must be important, I'd better follow him - even if it means going down a rabbit hole.

Ironically, when Alice and the Rabbit get to the croquet match, there's a boss shouting "Off with

71

their heads" – regardless of whether they arrive on time or not.

I start to think Scott Adams, of Dilbert fame, was right when he queried the concept of time management. "You can't win. Get things under control and they'll only give you more to do."

We are becoming a nation of White Rabbits. Always coming from somewhere, heading somewhere else, never present. Stress has become fashionable, self-induced and something people boast about. Sometimes it seems 'Business' is Busy-ness.

The need to be perpetually busy can lead to lower levels of productivity. Too often we engage in make-work projects, meetings for the sake of meetings, phone calls to cross-check emails that concern the faxes we sent. We need to be seen to be doing, and are often doing to be seen. We work hard, but we don't always work smart.

Being over worked can lead to stress, which can make us ill. The human body isn't built like the White Rabbit's. The amount of continual stress we experience is now considered the major life style factor in whether we will get one of the biggies - cancer, stroke or heart disease. Stress creates high levels of cortisol adrenaline. The body will eventually build a tolerance thus requiring even more and more. Stress is addictive, and stress will kill.

It isn't right or natural to be on a treadmill that is constantly moving faster than we are. Step off the treadmill and, like Alice, you will find it curiouser and curiouser. You will see that much of our stress is self-induced, and it is something over which we have control.

Next time you are late, consider cancelling rather than rushing. If there isn't much to do, take a break. Give yourself license to chill. Beware of the queen who is constantly threatening 'off with your head'. This kind of boss doesn't understand that you won't get much done if are running around like a headless chicken!

Be as calm as the Cheshire cat and you'll always find something to smile about.

PEARL OF BIZDOM
19

TEND AND BEFRIEND

Equality in the workplace is great but we cannot deny that men and woman are different.

19

Polly puts the kettle on

Recently I learned something that has profoundly changed my speeches and seminars. Just when I thought I had a firm understanding of stress management, I learned a simple, but profound fact. Women respond to stress differently than men.

We have all observed that when women get stressed they might put the kettle on, clean up, or phone a friend. When men get stressed their response is quite different. Men will often isolate themselves, retreat and shut down or in some cases, strike out. I thought these differences were due to society, conditioning and cultural norms. But then I unearthed a very interesting study.

In their landmark research, Drs. Laura Klein and Shelley Taylor at UCLA discovered the gender differences aren't just learned behaviours; they are linked to our biochemistry.

Drs. Klein and Taylor were joking about stress and gender when they had a classic 'aha' moment. Up until this point science had viewed stress as an ancient survival mechanism, left over from the time we were chased across the planet by sabre-toothed tigers. No one questioned the notion that stress was a modern version of "fight or flight."

But, queried our two scientists, where did stress responses such as tidying our desks, having a friendly chat or making a cup of tea fit in? They did a little research and discovered that 90% of stress studies had been done on men.

Klein and Taylor went on to conduct the first extensive study on women and stress. It suggests women have a larger behavioural repertoire in response to stress than men. A stressed woman can release cortisol (fight or flight adrenaline) but she is more likely to release oxytocin. Oxytocin, buffers cortisol, reducing its potentially aggressive effects; and it encourages women to nurture, organize and gather with other women. Oxytocin is sometimes called the cuddly chemical and its effect on behaviour has been affectionately named "tend and befriend."

In the workplace, it is important that we allow women to follow their instincts. Allowing them to "tend and befriend" will release oxytocin and quickly negate the ill effects of stress. Unfortunately some managers may perceive tidying and watering the plants as wasted time, but these activities are a more efficient way for a female to regain balance and increase focus and efficiency. Allowing this stress relief will positively affect health, productivity, and morale.

"Tend and befriend" may explain why women consistently outlive men. Study after study has found that social ties reduce our risk of diseases by lowering blood pressure, heart rate, and cholesterol. There is no doubt that friends help us live longer. The famed Nurse's Health Study from Harvard Medical School concluded that not having close friends or confidantes was as detrimental to your health as smoking or carrying extra weight.

Men too have oxytocin, but are unlikely to release it during stress - the male response is fight or flight. As fight is not an option in most workplaces, men tend to withdraw. Sharing stresses is perceived as a sign of weakness. This thinking leads to poor relationships, lack of communication and an increase, rather than relief, of stress.

Men should be encouraged to imitate their female counterparts' coping mechanisms. Men can condition their bodies to use oxytocin by doing something nurturing, such as making a cup of tea or having a chat at the water cooler.

Colleagues should know that when stress rears its ugly head, it's not friendship we should put on the back burner – it's the kettle.

PEARL OF BIZDOM
20

GIVING JUSTIFIES MAKING A LIVING

Charity events are necessary to keep good causes going. And they provide an excellent way to build team spirit.

78

Give at the office

This year HumourUs is going to organize its first charity event. Bill and I often sponsor people or take part ourselves in events, but this will be the first we organize as a business.

In my work with large organizations I have observed the role of charity. Invariably, businesses that put charity in a central role have happier employees than businesses where charity doesn't factor in. If it's good enough for the big companies, surely our little band at HumourUs will benefit too.

It is important to choose the right charity and the right event. Some companies will pick a charity and do events all year for this one charity. This can create relationships and tangible rewards. Other companies will choose a charity that is relevant to a staff member, or a charity that is local. Bill and I chose our charity because they are clients but also because our little event will be easy to plan and it will contribute to a much larger international day. We are going to host a coffee morning in aid of the World's Biggest Coffee Morning, for Macmillan Cancer Relief.

Charity, which begins at home, must be encouraged to continue, grow and flourish in the workplace. The perks go far beyond the coffee pot. Team building, improving morale and reaching targets are all spin-off benefits in addition to the money raised. Shared charity efforts make us proud to contribute, and the pride is tangible. By sponsoring a colleague cycling through Vietnam for a mental health charity, or supporting a posse walking the Great Wall of China for an inner city farm, we make a difference.

Workplace charity compliments corporate social responsibility. It is grassroots and personal, individuals or small teams can contribute. It doesn't require policies or strategies from the administration. Charity provides a great opportunity to socialize and feel part of a community, local or global.

There is little quantifiable research to determine charity's added value to a business. But I like that; it means we give for giving's sake, human to human. This humanity is underlined when a charity is chosen because of the personal passions and concerns of individuals in a workplace. This passion about a specific charity can help flush out new leaders amongst a team.

The lack of facts and figures about the benefits quiets my voice of the expert. My authority is anecdotal. In my observation, the most successful businesses with the happiest staff are those who choose to give. They do it collectively, they do it individually. They just do it. 'I gave at the office' is no longer a cynical excuse, but has become a statement of pride.

There is one statistic I can share from my research. The British people donate more per capita to charity than any other country in the world. We are the world's biggest givers. I don't know how that affects our economy and our bottom lines. I don't really care. In this case, simply knowing that Brits are generous makes me glad that this is where I do business.

Kate Hull Rodgers

PEARL OF BIZDOM
21

TIP THE SCALES TO ACHIEVE
WORK-LIFE BALANCE

*If attending a funeral is an okay excuse for time off,
then shouldn't a celebration be a good reason too?*

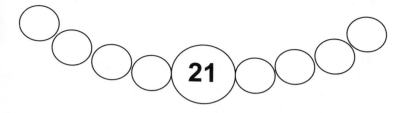

21

Getting into bed with balance

Big Brother called. No, not the television show, and not Orwell's creation. My big brother, Jim, who lives in Canada.

"How are things, Jim?"

"Not good, Kate, not good."

He called to say my family had a pow wow. My decision not to attend my sister's wedding - because I was too busy - hadn't gone down well. "Too much work," he declared, "Is not a good enough excuse. Not when it comes to family. You came for Mom's funeral, now come for Sharon's wedding."

Put like that, I saw his point. I agreed to make time somehow, and be there for the wedding. I would do the pop star thing, jet in and jet out.

But I soon discovered 'too much family' is not a good enough excuse; not when it comes to work.

Earlier in the year I needed to postpone work in order to attend my mother's funeral. I received immediate sympathy, and understanding. But when I called my clients to cancel obligations for my sister's wedding I elicited mystified silences.

Phoning in sick was valid, but phoning in well wasn't.

As a consultant teaching about work-life balance, I have come to realize that we often need a helping hand in attaining that balance. Research shows that businesses with low absenteeism, high staff retention, and healthy bottom lines have developed workplace policies that tip the scales in favour of life.

One strategy that is popular in North America is called Duvet Days. Allowing Duvet Days means that staff are permitted, without question, to phone in well.

At first glance this may seem like a new-fangled fad. Companies may be reluctant to offer Duvet Days because employees might exploit the privilege. And what about customer-facing companies? It wouldn't do to hear an announcement: "The 8:15 train is cancelled because the driver decided to have a lie in…"

Duvet Days should be implemented with discretion. Boundaries are set by limiting the number of days allotted. Interestingly, surveys contradict employer's fears as often these allotted 'ays are not taken. Duvet Days build mutual trust nd there is a marked increase in staff morale.

Staff should have a strategy to forewarn 'eagues. This "planned absenteeism" has a or benefit. There is a welcomed decline in rise" days off, when an employee calls in sick morning and colleagues suddenly have to

Duvet Days are flexible. When a workplace has to be met, often it's all hands on deck.

People's personal time may be sacrificed for work. But when the deadline has been met, and there is a momentary lull, and the duvet beckons... Taking a day or morning off will help restore the balance. Employees are more likely to undertake long days without resentment, knowing they will be rewarded with time to rest and recuperate.

On my return from my sister's wedding, I worked harder to keep my clients happy. My family relations are stronger, my work relations are stronger.

To achieve work-life balance we often need to tip the scales in favour of life. After all, Big Brother is watching!

PEARL OF BIZDOM
22

MAKE YOURSELF SCARCE

Don't just be fashionably late, try not showing up at all.

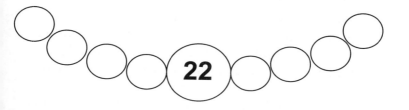

The Garbo Principle

I didn't invent it, but I've named it. I imagine the phrase appearing in many future business books - "The Garbo Principle" as first coined by Humour Specialist, Kate Hull Rodgers.

The Garbo Principle - *"I vant to be alone"* - is the art of the anti-sell. When you make yourself unavailable, everyone wants a piece of you. If you position your product as a rare diamond, you'll command a gem of a price.

I first encountered the idea of anti-sell in Canada, while working in theatre. A lighting designer had a business card that simply read: "Ask Around." No name, no contact information. It was cocky, confident and cunning. It was also intriguing. Anyone who did ask around discovered his reputation was so exemplary that everyone had his contact details. By being unforthcoming he had the entire theatre community giving him references and passing on his information. And, I ask you, how many business cards do you remember 20 years later?

I've also seen the practice of anti-sell in Britain. I was especially impressed with the marketing materials of one of my own competitors. Their brochure included fabulous descriptions of services and rave reviews from clients and the proviso "If you like us – and if we like you..." How confident to say you're not prepared to work with just anybody.

Anti-sell, I think, can only occur when your services are well established. I was confident enough to risk it recently with an important client.

I had a meeting with a Divisional Manager of a major multi-national. If she hired me for the event we were discussing it could lead to much lucrative work for HumourUs. The manager outlined her agenda for the event, and then asked what I could add.

"Nothing," I replied.

"Nothing?"

This was my big moment to make my sales pitch, but I chose to not just undersell, but to anti-sell. "Nothing," I repeated.

She was thoughtful. The she looked at her agenda, and crossed out three items. "Now what could you add?"

"A lot." I said. And together we proceeded to plan an event to which my contribution was central, not an addition.

I took a risk that paid off. I got the job and lots of rewarding work with this client has come to fruition as well.

There have been successful advertising campaigns by Pot Noodle and Beechams who tried to convince us how awful they taste.

More recently, we had the hit band, Arctic Monkeys, refuse to show up at the Brit Awards or to play on Top of the Pops. Their no-show caused an avalanche of new sales for their album. Front page headlines declared them bigger than the Beatles - who you'll recall were bigger than Jesus.

It is human nature to want what we can't have. Your customers are human. So sometimes, if they want something – don't give it to them. Try The Garbo Principle instead.

PEARL OF BIZDOM
23

MAKE A LIST

Often it's the simplest things that can help the most.

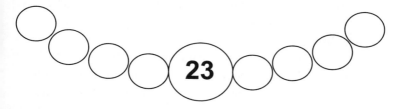

Countdown to the joy of lists

I love to make lists. They are so easy, so clear, so helpful, and yet often they aren't appreciated as a strategic tool for business and personal development.

For years I had been making To Do lists and shopping lists. But it wasn't until I was hospitalized for mental health reasons that I was introduced to another kind of list.

It was during a group therapy session lead by the ward Occupational Therapist. "Today," she began, "We are going to write a Joy List." I was in a long term psychiatric unit; joy was not something we talked about. The silence was deafening. "For this exercise," she explained, "Joy will be defined as things or activities that sustain your desire to be alive." On her flipchart, in bright red felt-tip, she wrote: Joy List. But the silence was now defiant; her white page remained blank until the session finished.

I was intrigued. I couldn't help but think Joys Lists must be powerful stuff. Otherwise we would have just done it.

Two years later I was out of hospital, rebuilding my life, baby step by baby step. I started a To Do list. I was surprised the first thing I wrote was: Make a Joy List.

I got a special journal and a special pen. I wrote Joy List at the top of the page and like the hospital therapist was poised to start writing. But nothing came. Each day I returned to the list and after 3 weeks there were only 2 things on it. The emptiness of the page only served to depress me.

I had to rethink my approach. I realized the exercise wasn't the issue; I was blocked because I was hung up on the word Joy. I believed that joy must be epic. I thought it meant having the perfect mate, the great job, the Porsche.

I decided to make joy less important and just answer the question "What brings me joy?"

I started with the premise that I must take joy in things I did often. Well, I ate a lot of cereal. Sultana Bran for breakfast, lunch, dinner and snacks. I added that to my list.

What else did I do a lot of…? I took a lot of hot baths. Wrote that down. I was glad to see I had doubled my list. I took a break for cereal and a bath.

Then I had a paradigm shift. Suddenly, I was surrounded by things that brought me joy. As I ate my cereal, I saw the newly painted kitchen, yellow, my favourite colour. In the bathroom, I touched my shell collection on the windowsill. It had been there forever, but now I saw it with new eyes, eyes that saw joy. My list grew quickly. It tripled and quadrupled. My Joy List soon filled many pages. The way I tell the story now; the sultana bran really freed me up.

As a speaker and trainer, I now stand next to the flipchart, and I teach and preach about the uses of Lists. They can help clarify where we have been, where we are, and where we are going.

A popular business application is a SWOT, an exercise listing strengths, weaknesses, opportunities and threats. Another idea is a Countdown using Stop, Start, Continue, – list 3 things you are going to stop, 2 things you are going to start and 1 thing you are going to continue.

If you use To Do lists, don't forget to try To Done lists; celebrate achievements.

Past, present, future. Lists are a great reminder of the simple but profound exercise of taking stock. And the process itself is a joy.

PEARL OF BIZDOM
24

DON'T THINK TWICE,
SAY SOMETHING NICE

To compliment and be complimented is a thrill and a skill.

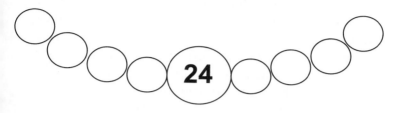

Kate Hull Rodgers

24

Well done

Flattery will get you everywhere. Everywhere is surely where we want to be. So why, I ask, don't we hear more compliments in the workplace?

Perhaps we have fear of appearing false when giving compliments. A gushy "missing you already" style doesn't sit well with the archetypal business reserve.

Perhaps when receiving compliments we are more comfortable self-deprecating. If we accept we feel we may appear big headed. Or perhaps we fear we might have to live up to high expectations.

Whatever the reason for our reluctance, it's time to get over it. Complimenting builds rapport, increases self-confidence and builds camaraderie among colleagues.

Moreover, it's easy – if you know how.

Complimenting has two elements, giving and receiving.

Receiving is simple. Start by breaking bad habits. Don't be one of those misguided people who upon receiving a compliment, kicks it back in the face of the giver. "That's a nice dress" should never be countered with "this old thing?" When someone compliments you on your great presentation, don't point out that one of your slides was unclear. Rejecting a compliment effectively tells the giver that their judgment is wrong. Odds are they will think twice about complimenting you again.

You should just say the two magic words: Thank you.

You can also use a technique called Reflecting or Deflecting. Reflecting is when you return the compliment - "thank you for noticing," or "thank you for saying so". Deflecting is when you receive the compliment, then share it with others. "Thank you, Susan helped me prepare the presentation."

The better you receive compliments, the more likely you are to get them. The more compliments you receive the better you feel about yourself, and your confidence increases.

The second element to complimenting is giving. It can take many forms. It is beneficial to expand the definition of what constitutes a compliment. Don't limit positive feedback to physical appearance or a job well done. Consider that when you are chatting with a colleague and your mobile rings, you compliment them by turning it off. When someone is working non-stop to make a deadline, compliment their efforts by surprising them with a cup of tea. The ultimate compliment you can give an associate is your focus, your time, and your attention. To listen is to compliment.

When giving compliments it is best to be honest. Say what you mean, and mean what you say.

Whether you graciously receive a compliment, or generously give one, it's all about making the other person feel valued.

Thank you for reading.

PEARL OF BIZDOM
25

AVOID AVOIDING

Sometimes when you put something off, it can really hurt.

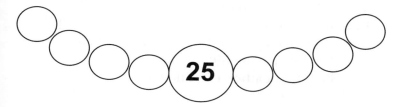

25

Breaking through the pain barrier

Throb, throb, throb. While some throbbing can be quite pleasurable, this pulsating is anything but pleasant. It is pain like I've never known. Ow, there it goes again. Throb, throb, throb. My toe is going to explode. This agony could have been avoided. That knowledge is like salt on my wound. If only I had dealt with the problem when it first occurred I wouldn't be enduring tortuous discomfort now. Life teaches us many lessons if we are prepared to listen. Today I am learning from my wart.

Diary of a Verruca:
March 6 - I notice a tiny bump under the skin of my right big toe. I remember the day well. I was at the pool. I recall looking with envy at the ladies who wore protective plastic sandals. I recall getting dressed ever so quickly. No one would know my shame.

April 26 - The tiny bump has broken through the skin. My toe is giving birth to a cauliflower. Don't want to think about it.

April 27 - I said I don't want to think about it.

June 4 – Someone treads on my foot, my yelp is disproportionately loud. I make a mental note to do something about "my little friend".

July 30 to September 15 - I do nothing.

September 16 - My husband asks if I am limping. I decide to tackle the problem.

October 26 - I buy some over-the-counter gel I must use daily.

October 26, 27, and 28 - I use said gel.

October 29 - January 2 - See July 30 to September 15

January 3 – Treating my wart is enough of a priority it has made my New Year's resolution list.

Over the next 14 months I use the daily gel weekly. I attend the monthly NHS Wart Clinic every second or third month; sometimes I manage two months in a row. I think about my wart a lot. I talk about it even more. I make little progress in getting rid of it, but have kept the problem at bay.

Finally because I've got two days off in a row and can afford to be out of commission, I make an appointment with the expert.

Paul, the chiropodist, has warm and gentle hands. The razor sharp scalpel he holds glints, giving his warm and gentle hands an aura of healing. Having scraped my little friend clean, he picks up a long, tubular contraption attached to a tank with no markings. Then he touches the long tubular contraption thingy to my wart. The pain is excruciating. Dentists' drills pass before my eyes. Paul asks gently how long I've had the wart. I confess that it's been two years. He tuts and says, "Shame. The sooner you treat the problem, the faster it heals."

Throb, throb, throb. Today, as I bask in pain, his words come back to me. The sooner you treat the problem, the faster it heals. This is a fundamental basic of time management. Too much time is lost avoiding problems, or only half-heartedly dealing with them. If they are left to fester, they will need more invasive treatment. When you write your To Do list, put the things you least want to tackle first, not last. The longer you leave a difficult task, the bigger it seems. Don't put off that difficult call you've been meaning to make. Make it and move on. Get it off your mind.

I believe life teaches us everything we need to know about business. I learned the lesson that avoiding pain creates more pain. It's a lesson I needed to learn, warts and all.

Kate Hull Rodgers

PEARL OF BIZDOM
26

KNOW THE WORTH OF MIRTH

But what kind of fun, and when?

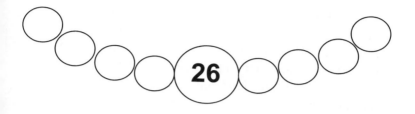

26

Fun isn't just for April Fools

There is a new business initiative in America called National Fun at Work Day. The Mayors of Dallas and San Francisco have officially sanctioned it. Many companies have embraced it. A firm in Kansas celebrated the day by turning its car park into a beach party, complete with trucked-in sand, live music and free sun glasses. 3000 employees of Chase Industries in 20 cities were provided with disposable cameras and told to go on photo safari. In Seattle, one company held a lottery to name floors of their office block after workers.

National Fun at Work Day is a wonderful idea, but it isn't enough. It runs the risk of trivializing fun with tokenism. To create an environment that encourages enjoyment in employment is much more complex than having a BBQ in the car park.

The goal is for fun to become a benchmark of success not an added extra. Fun must become entwined in the way we work. For this to happen, we must be clear on the value added to our lives and businesses. The benefits are now well documented.

They include improved morale, motivation, attendance and staff retention.

Fun Days are an excellent way to help an organization team build by creating shared memories. But when the frivolity is forced it can meet with resistance. Not everyone has the same idea of what is fun. Humour is a sense, and fun is a matter of taste.

I recently had first hand knowledge of this. You see, I don't like practical jokes. This is my personal taste not my professional opinion. Practical jokes, in the right context, can be wonderful workplace fun. Just not my workplace, please. Bill, my husband and business partner, loves practical jokes. He recently sent me a memo saying that my wages would be docked 2 hours for doing laundry during work time. It took me a minute to realize he was joking. I didn't find this funny, and told him so.

"I think it's very funny," he said. "You're the Humour Specialist, are you going to censor my idea of fun?"

My professional side knows he has a valid point. My job is to encourage people to exercise their idea of fun, not judge it. But my personal side still thinks my husband's a bit of a chump.

Your kinda fun, my kinda fun, our kinda fun – it's a minefield we must navigate. Respecting and tolerating other peoples' ideas of fun is the challenge many businesses don't want to take on. Instead of allowing fun to become the fibre of a workplace, it is often relegated to specific activities such as Dress Down Friday or a DVD lunch hour. Interweaving fun and allowing it to grow organically will increase productivity and well being. It is a healthy diverse organization that will allow fun in its many guises. Every day should be a Fun at Work day, and it is not just in April we should be Fools.

PEARL OF BIZDOM
27

TALK THE TALK

Language, like technology, never stands still.
It isn't jargon, it's communication.

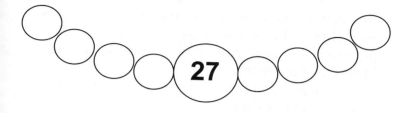

27

It's all in the translation

I look back in horror to my first networking event. I was so green.

Seven of us sat at a round table, each given two minutes to pitch our products. I'd little business experience, but I could bluff. The gentleman next to me pitched his company and at one minute forty-five concluded, "I work in HR." "Haitch Are?" I asked. "Is that nearby?"

I wasn't trying to be funny. I seriously thought it was a place. Mind you, when I first moved to the UK I didn't know Stella Artois was a beer, I thought she was a rich woman who patronized the arts.

My Haitch Are query caused six heads to slowly turn in my direction. Networking can be tough, and I wanted to slide under the table. My bluff had been called. I tried so hard to appear 'in the know,' but now found myself firmly in the no-no.

Early in my career I was determined I would never speak in jargon or TLAs – three letter abbreviations. But I've learned that jargon, and short hand can be effective communication tools.

Jargon is only jargon to the uninitiated. My first networking event taught me that Personnel is now Human Resources. This is shortened to HR, pronounced Haitch Are. You, of course, already knew that, but I didn't.

Jargon is not meant to intimidate. It's just a quick way to talk the talk.

Much of the new lingo is just the old lingo rehashed. Staff are colleagues, meetings are forums, targets are plans, and brainstorming is a thought shower. Jargon is the constant evolution of business language.

The use of some "new" language allows an element of venting and letting off steam, without offending. Here are a few favourites I've collected -

1. **BLAMESTORMING** – Sitting around in a group, discussing why a deadline was missed or a project failed, and who was responsible.

2. **MOUSE POTATO** – The on-line, wired generation's answer to the couch potato.

3. **SITCOM** – Single Income, Two Children, Oppressive Mortgage. What yuppies turn into when they have children and one of them stops working to stay home with the kids. Can no longer relate to DINK friends (Double Income No Kids).

4. **SEAGULL MANAGER** – A manager who flies in, makes a lot of noise, craps on everything, then leaves.

5. **STRESS PUPPY** – A person who thrives on being stressed out and whiney.

6. **ASSMOSIS** – Absorbing success by kissing up to the boss rather than working hard.

7. **GARBO PRINCIPLE** – First coined by Kate Hull Rodgers, it is the art of the anti-sell.

8. **PERCUSSIVE MAINTENANCE** – The fine art of whacking an electronic device to get it working.

9. **SALMON DAY** – Spending an entire day swimming upstream only to get screwed and die.

10. **ADMINISPHERE** – The rarefied organizational layers beginning just above the common worker. Decisions that fall from the adminisphere are often profoundly inappropriate or irrelevant to the problems they were designed to solve. This is often affiliated with the dreaded "administrivia" - needless paperwork and processes.

Kate Hull Rodgers

PEARL OF BIZDOM
28

CHOOSE YOUR NEWS

Information overload is a modern day syndrome that can affect our sense of well being. Sometimes the cure is to detox and fast for a while.

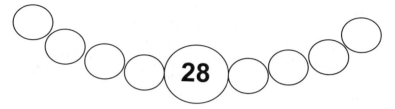

28

No news is good

"Hurry boys, let's get out of here!"

"What?"

"I said LET'S ROLL!!!!!"

Not until I saw the look of fear on my son Harvey's face did I realize how panicked I must sound. When my younger boy Dominic began to cry, I knew I had a problem.

The problem is that I have developed a heightened sense of fear. Fear developed from reading and watching too much news.

My present panic was set off by an unusual event at the swimming pool. The boys and I were at the pool getting changed out of our bathing costumes, when suddenly I heard all sorts of banging. Peaking out from the change cubicle I saw the staff conducting a locker search. Hurriedly they opened and closed every locker. I heard one woman report into her walkie-talkie, "I haven't found anything, we'd better hurry."

With the bang of a locker and a flash of my highly developed imagination, I immediately understood the situation. This was a bomb threat. At first I was very calm. I quickly deduced they hadn't informed the general public, as they didn't want to cause unnecessary chaos. I knew my boys and I were going to be lucky survivors. I knew exactly what to do. I had spent the morning pouring over the HM Government manifesto Preparing for Emergencies that serendipitously dropped through the mail slot. I visualized myself talking to CNN recounting our narrow escape, my boys at my side with soot on their faces...

But my reverie was broken by another locker banging. That's when I panicked. That's when Dominic began wailing. He caught the attention of the pool attendant. She stopped her search, and I was able to ask for a progress report.

"There's not much hope." she said. I shivered. I prepared myself for the imminent evacuation. But the attendant continued, "A girl's left her mobile," then added, with great self-importance, "We've got to find it quick, or somebody'll lift it."

Oh.

The pool water on my skin turned to a cold sweat. I realized I'm not informed, I'm paranoid. One loud bang in a public place and I'm exclaiming "let's roll" as if I were in the midst of a terrorist attack.

Can you blame me? I believe it is necessary that I am never uninformed, unprepared, under false impressions... but is it?

A little knowledge is a dangerous thing, but equally detrimental to our health is the modern-day dilemma known as information overload. Overload occurs when we are bombarded and lose the ability to sift what is important and pertinent. Since the intensive reporting of 9/11, the Iraq War, 7/7, and the tsunami, mental health organizations have reported a sharp increase in anxiety caused by news. Workplace research shows that following a catastrophe reported in the news, there is an increase in absenteeism, and a decrease in efficiency. This continuous state of heightened anxiety affects health and productivity.

News, now available 24/7 and in more mediums than ever before, can be an addiction just like caffeine, smoking, or sugar. The cure, as with most stress, is simple. Take back the control. (Yes, the remote control!)

Personally, I am breaking the news habit, completely. I am now on a self-induced news blackout. No TV, no newspapers, no discussions. When I'm ready, I will begin to reintroduce information. I will tune in selectively. For my re-entry I'll probably start with Reader's Digest.

I regain my perspective on world events by remembering a simple phrase - Choose Your News.

In Closing…

Funnily, I seem to have finished where I began – at the swimming pool. Having made this cyclic journey, I wonder if I am any wiser. I think so. By sharing my stories and extracting the lessons, I've recognized that experience can be a struggle but it is the greatest teacher.

From the start, my goal with Pearls of Bizdom has been to write a business book that I'd like to read. I certainly hope you've enjoyed reading it, too. And that, like me, you've come to appreciate:

Grit is great when it becomes a Pearl.

Lots of Laughter

Kate Hull Rodgers

.